VOICES OF THE SEA

Voices of the Sea
A Dream Series

Patricia Feinman

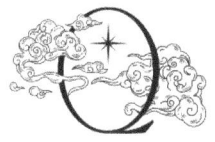

Querencia Press – Chicago IL

Q AN IMPRINT OF QUERENCIA PRESS

© Copyright 2024

Patricia Feinman

All Rights Reserved

No reproduction, copy or transmission of this publication may be made without written permission.
No paragraph of this publication may be reproduced, copied or transmitted save with the written permission of the author.

Any person who commits any unauthorized act in relation to this publication may be liable to criminal prosecution and civil claims for damages.

ISBN 978 1 963943 24 5

www.querenciapress.com

First Published in 2024

Querencia Press, LLC
Chicago IL

Printed & Bound in the United States of America

For Art

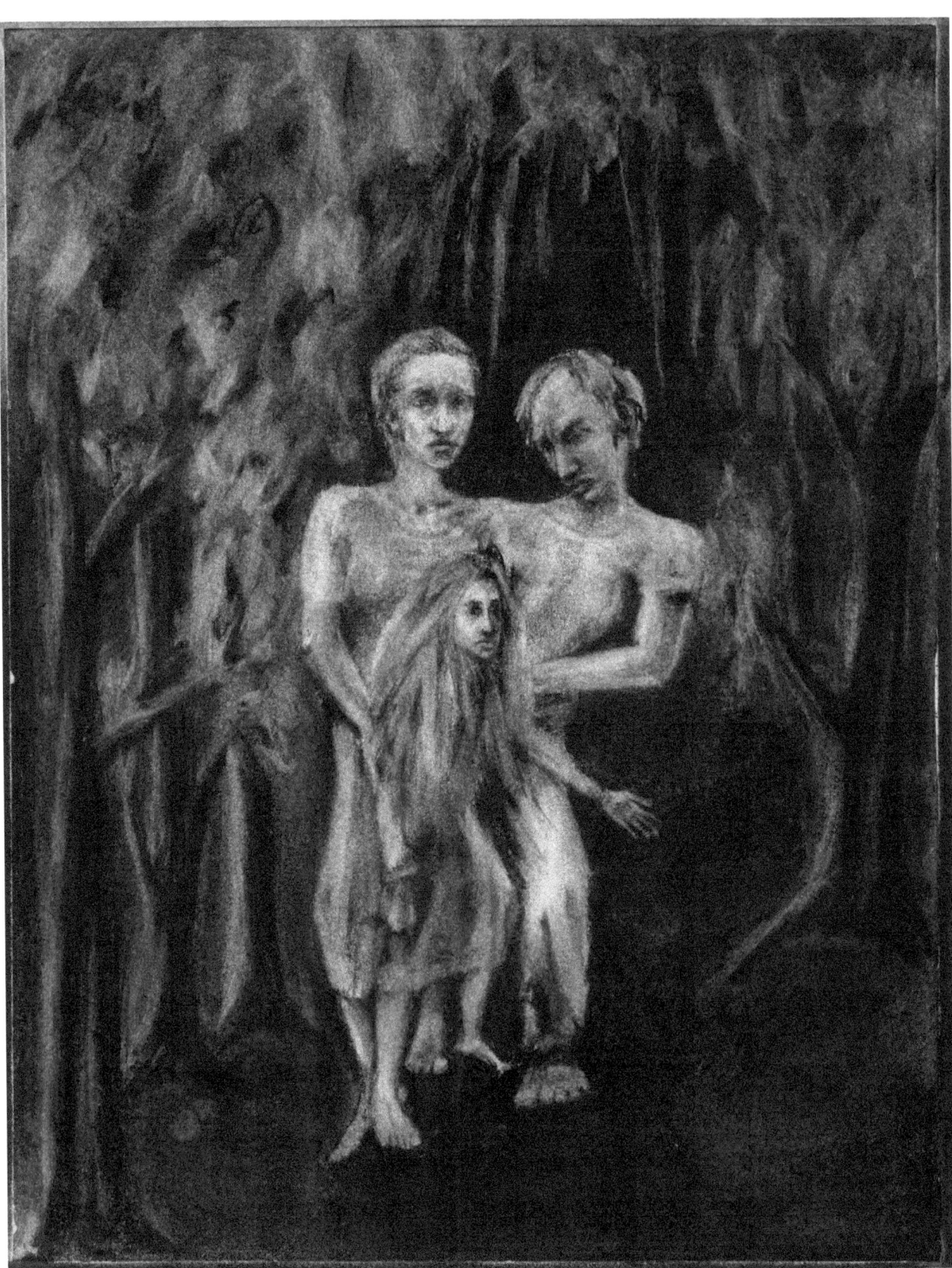

We seem to have been here before, we say,

The melody sounds so familiar.

But the undercurrents have changed

And the voices sing in a slightly lower key.

We prepare for the changing tide.

The voices whisper in our ears

But we can't understand the words,

The pressure of the water deafens us.

Can we ride this wave much longer, we ask.

As we try to sink our fingers in,

The water trickles through them,

Rushing around our bodies.

We dance to the music of the voices.

As the waves lull us to sleep.

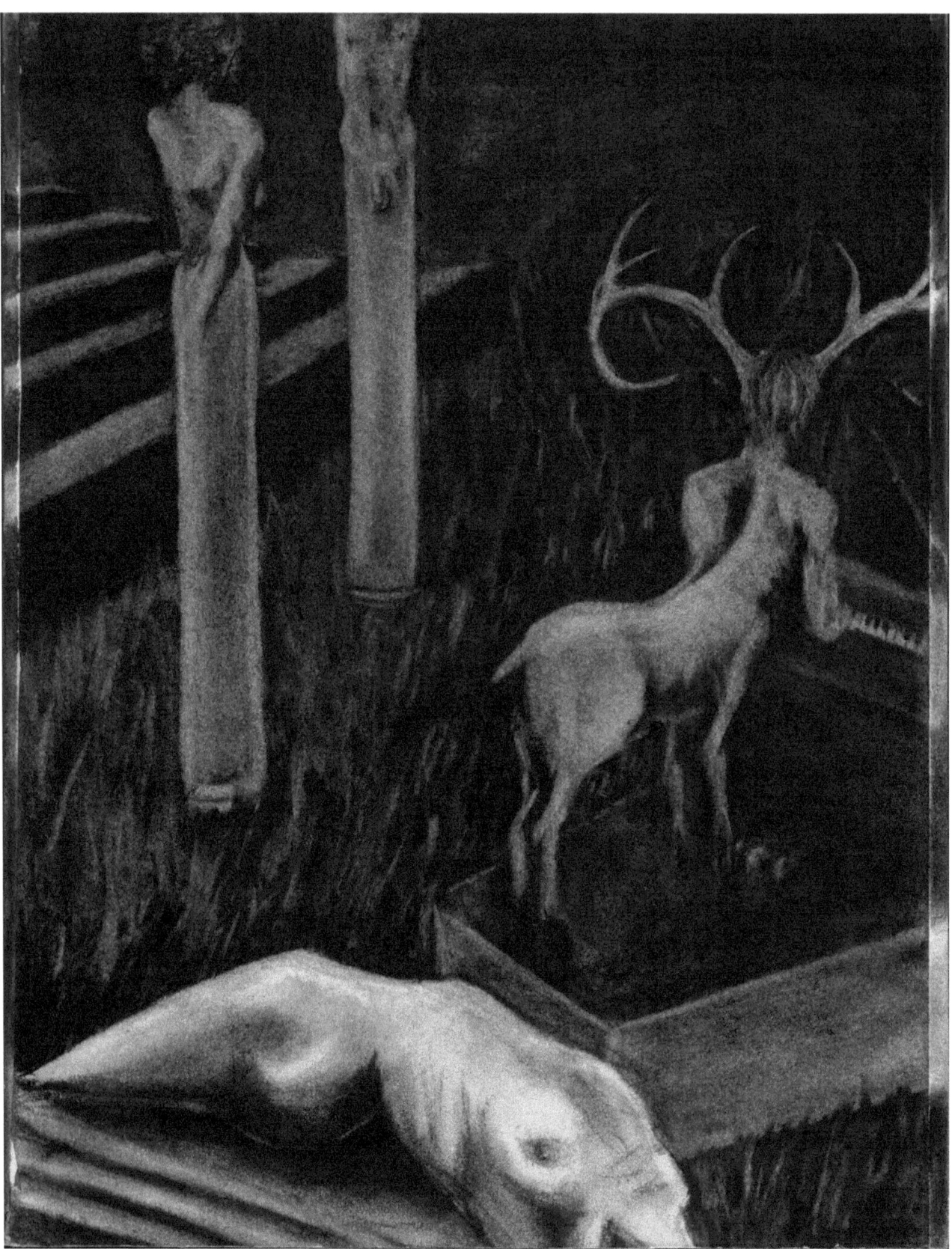

And we dream that we are standing on the shore.

We dream that the wind caresses us,

We dream that the sun is shining on us,

That we can see the sky.

As the sun dries our dripping bodies,

We see the ocean,

Shimmering in the distance,

We hear the voices plaintive cry.

We don't need to understand the words,

The voices blend with the wind so beautifully.

We watch the sea crashing against the rock-face,

And suddenly, we are awake.

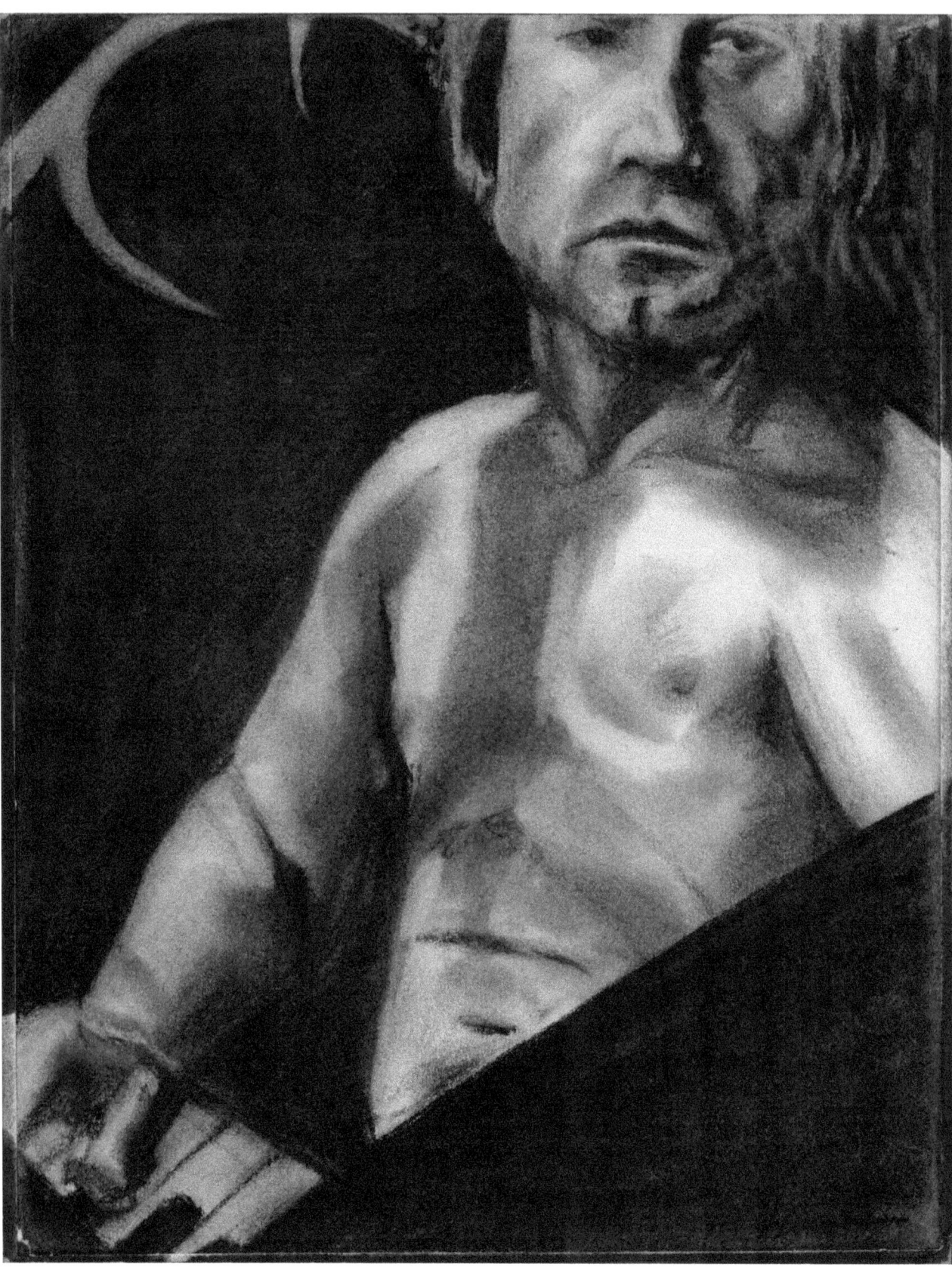

Where are we now,

We ask each other

As we try to stand up,

And we can no longer see the sky.

We are rolled over and over in the waves again,

Clasping each other's hands.

Where are we now,

We ask the voices.

But the voices only say

That they are hungry, cold.

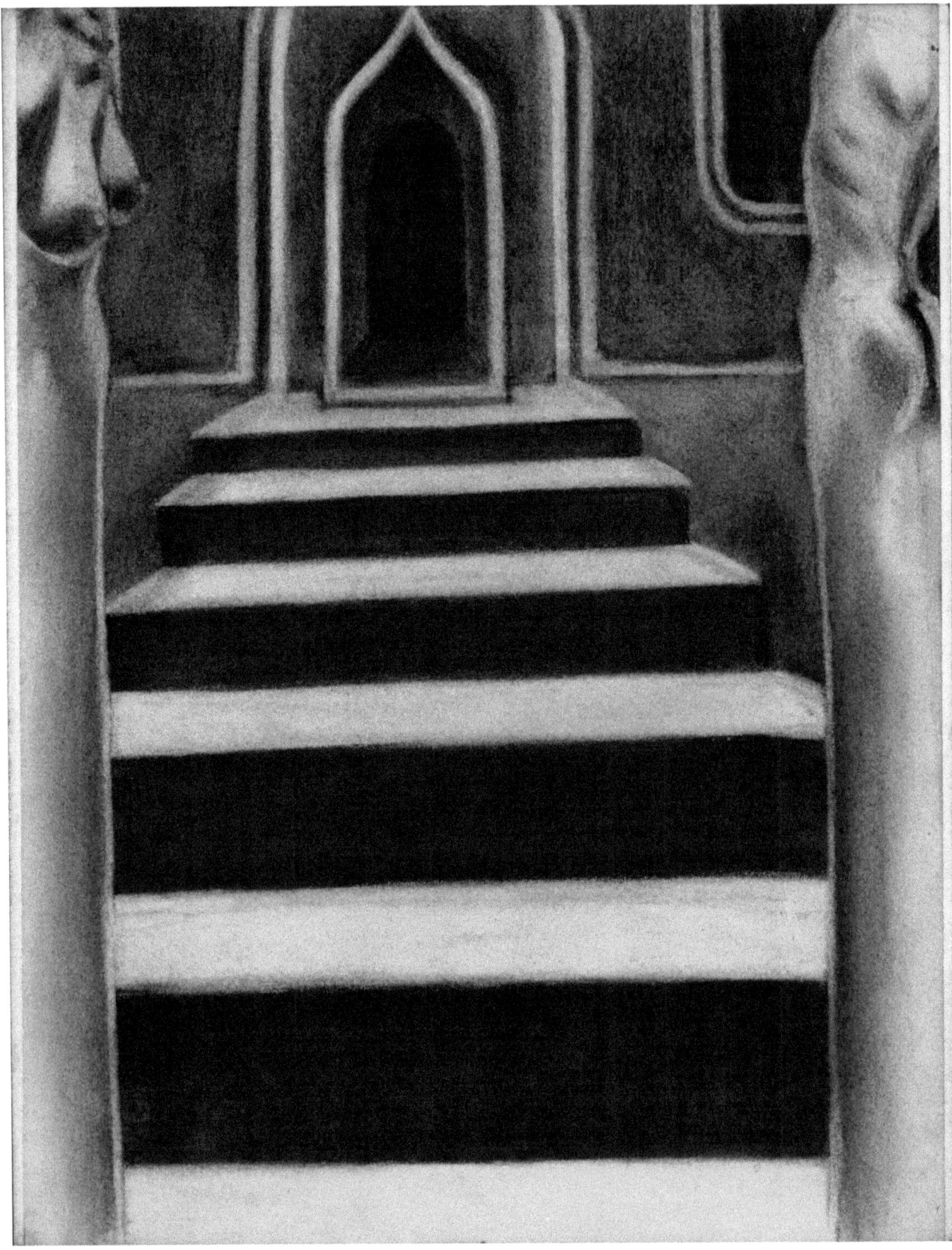

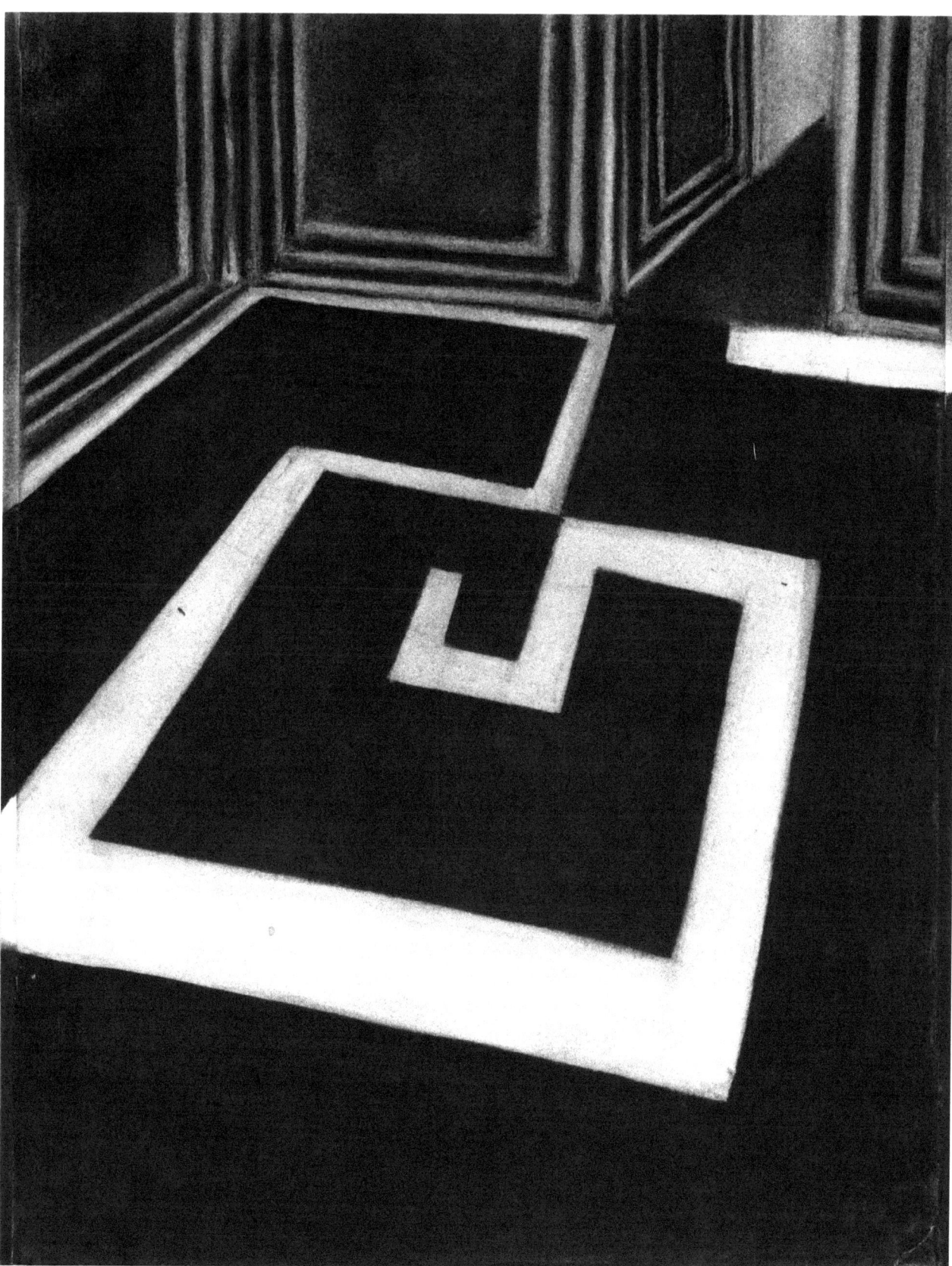

We can barely remember the feel of solid ground,

The caress of the sun,

The deep, deep blue of the sky.

Where is the sky, we ask the voices

And they mournfully say,

You're in the sky

You're in the sky,

And we call them liars.

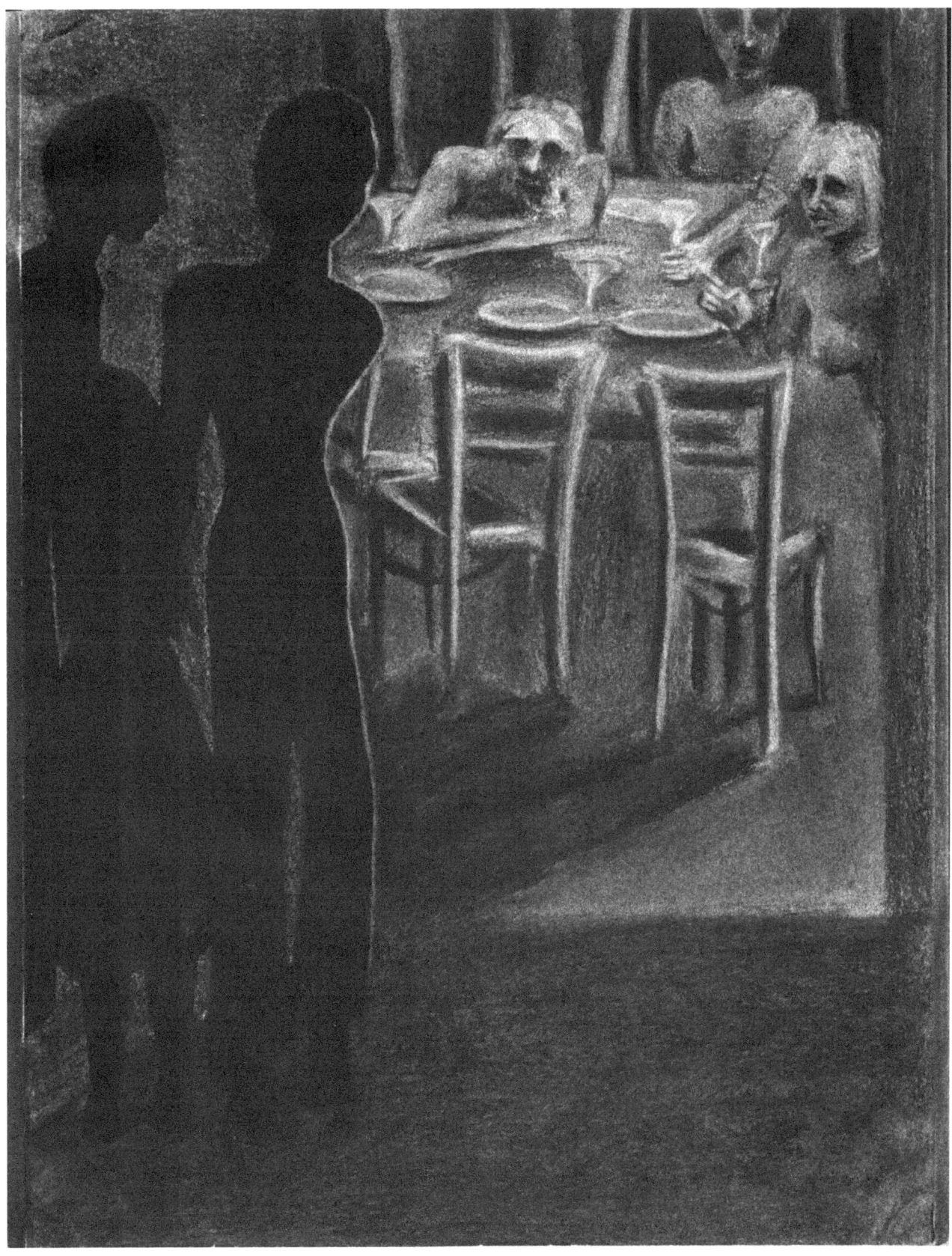

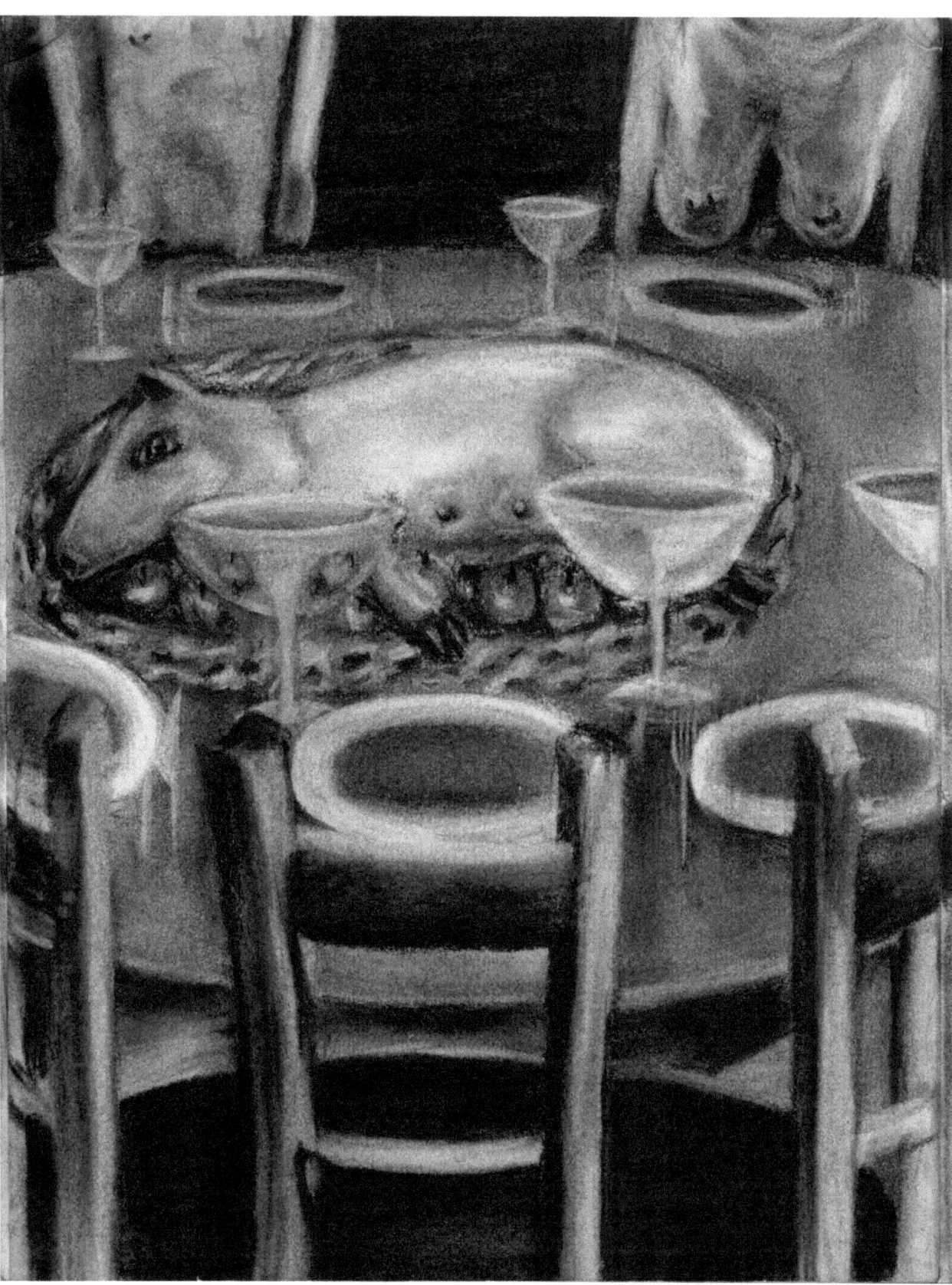

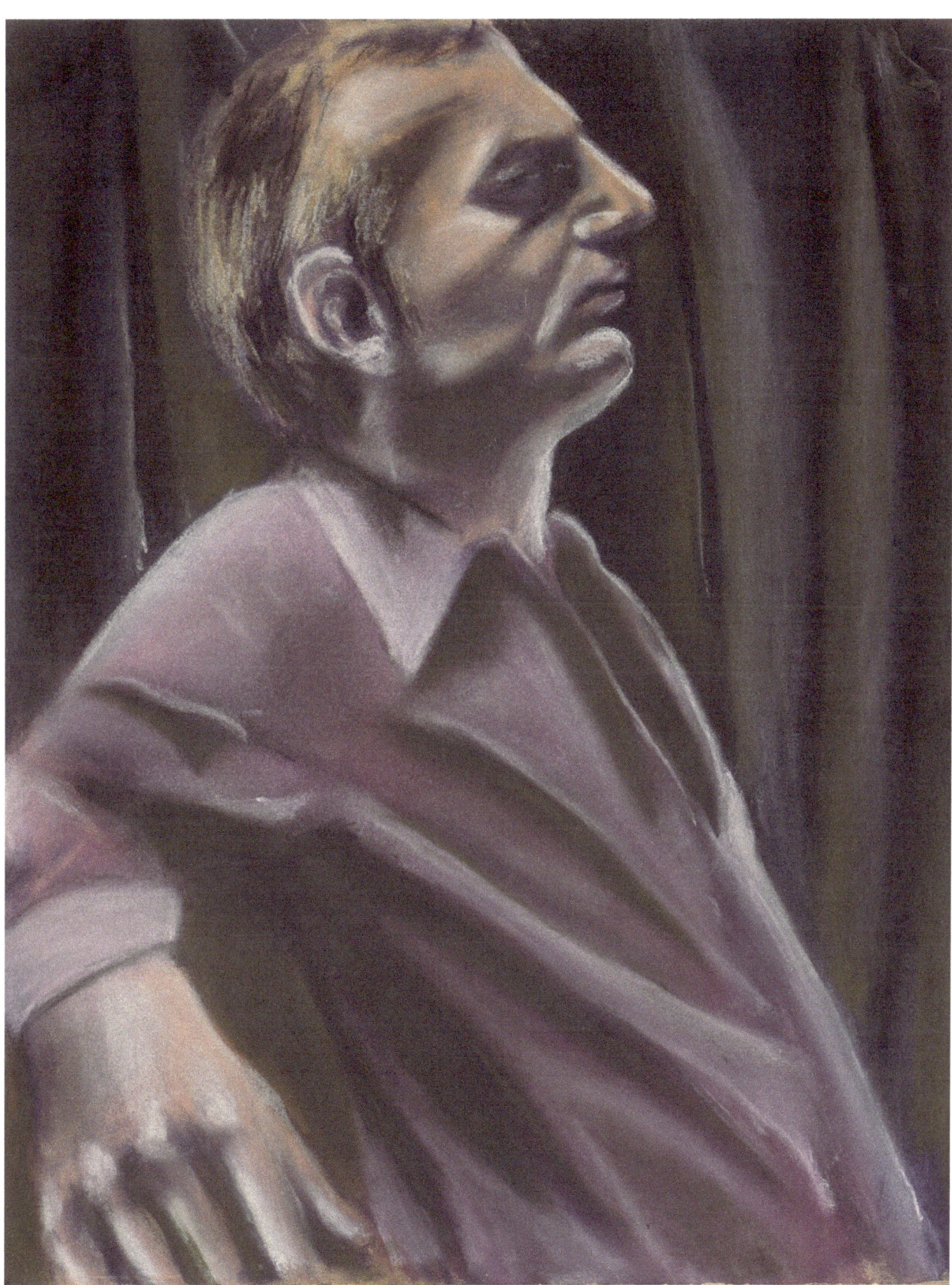

But is there a shore, we ask ourselves.

Is there a sun and sky?

We were only dreaming after all.

Dreamers Dreamers Dreamers,

Chant the voices.

This is all there is

This is all there is.

We are caught in the rhythm

Of a monotonous melody,

Repeated chords,

G's and D's and G's and D's

And we sleep.

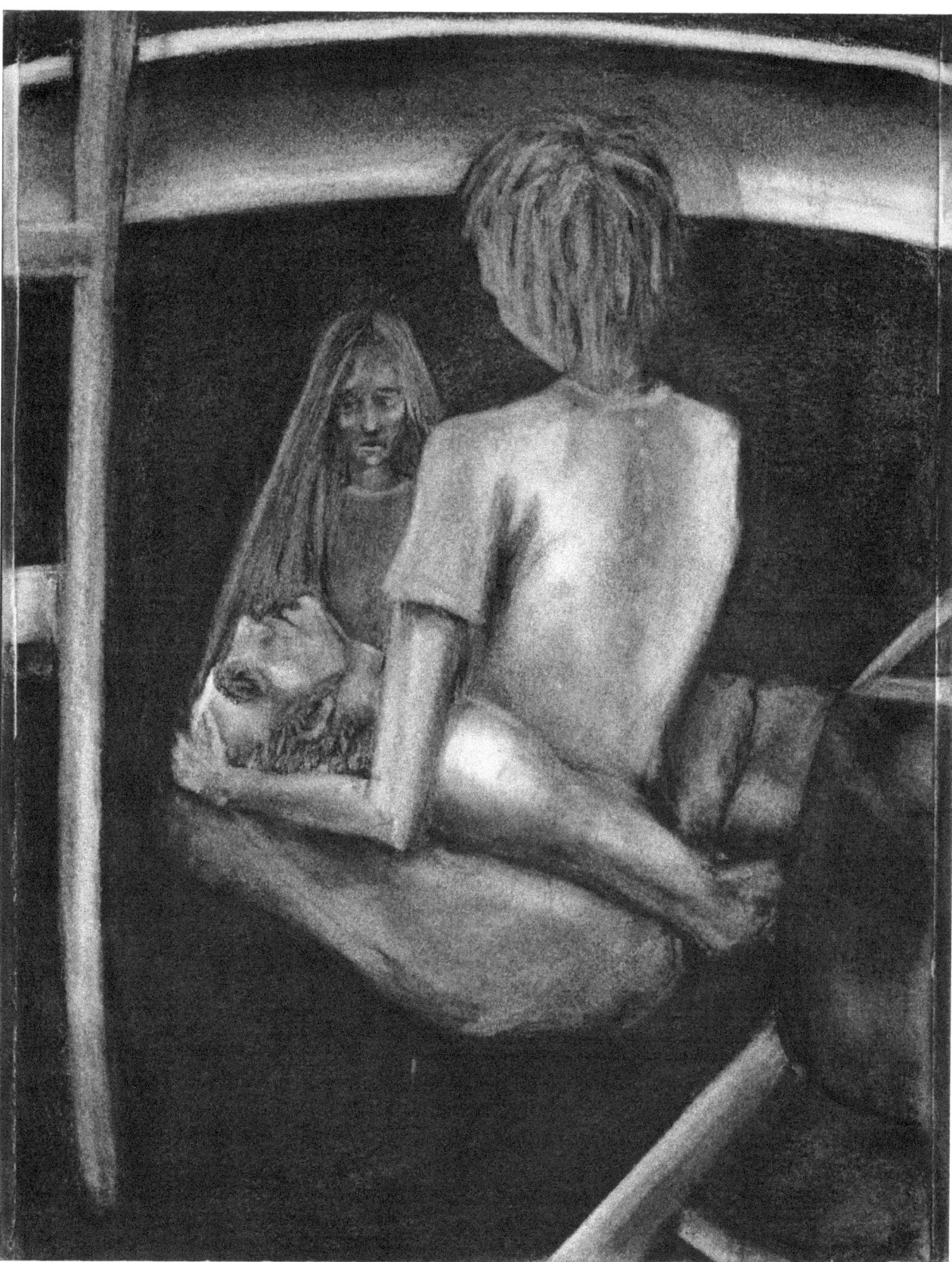

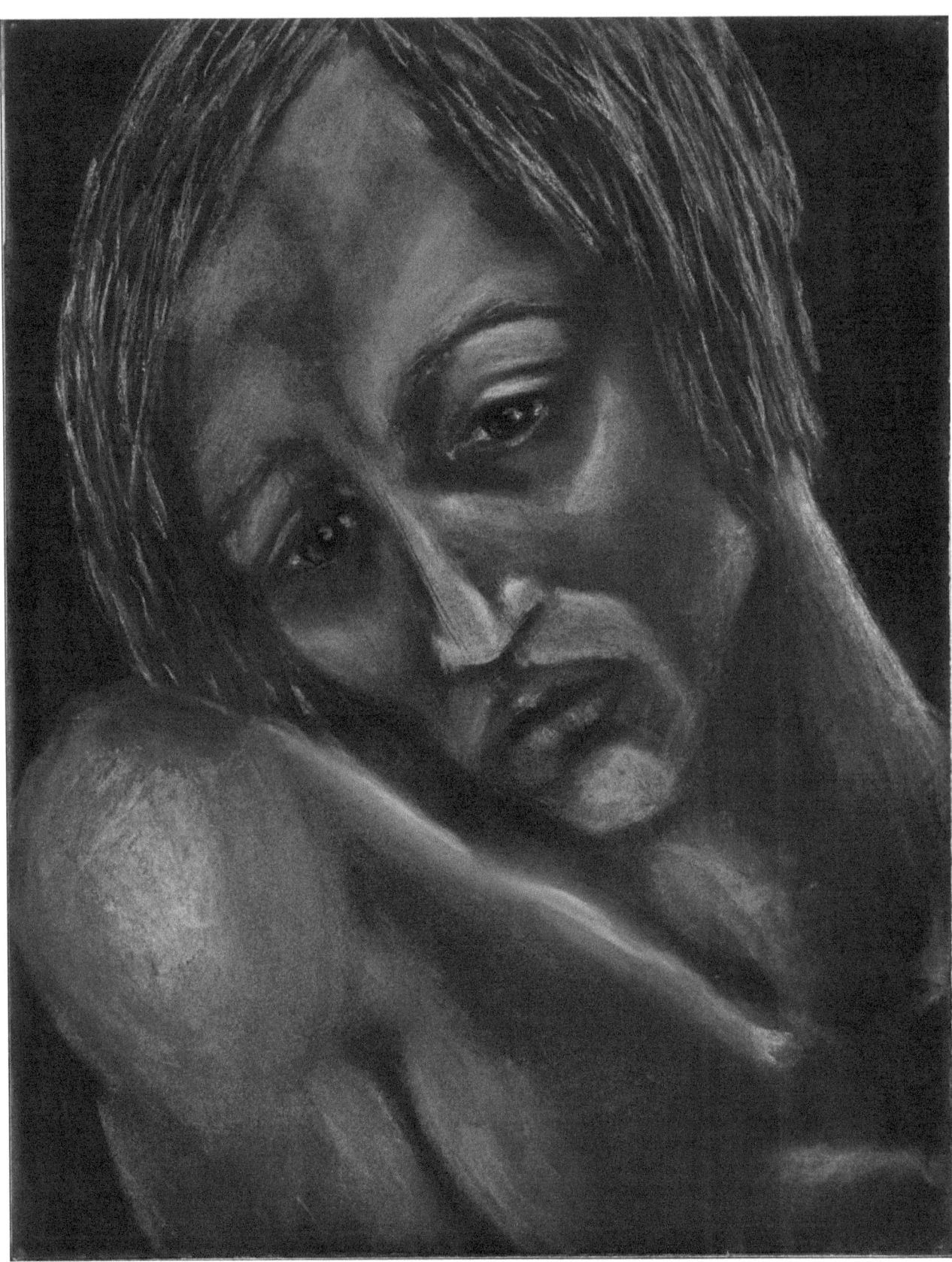

And we dream

That we have reached the ocean floor.

Around us it is silent, still

As a mountain of shifting sands rises before us.

We are the ocean floor,

We are the shifting sands,

We are the mountain,

Until the waves crash against us

And we wake.

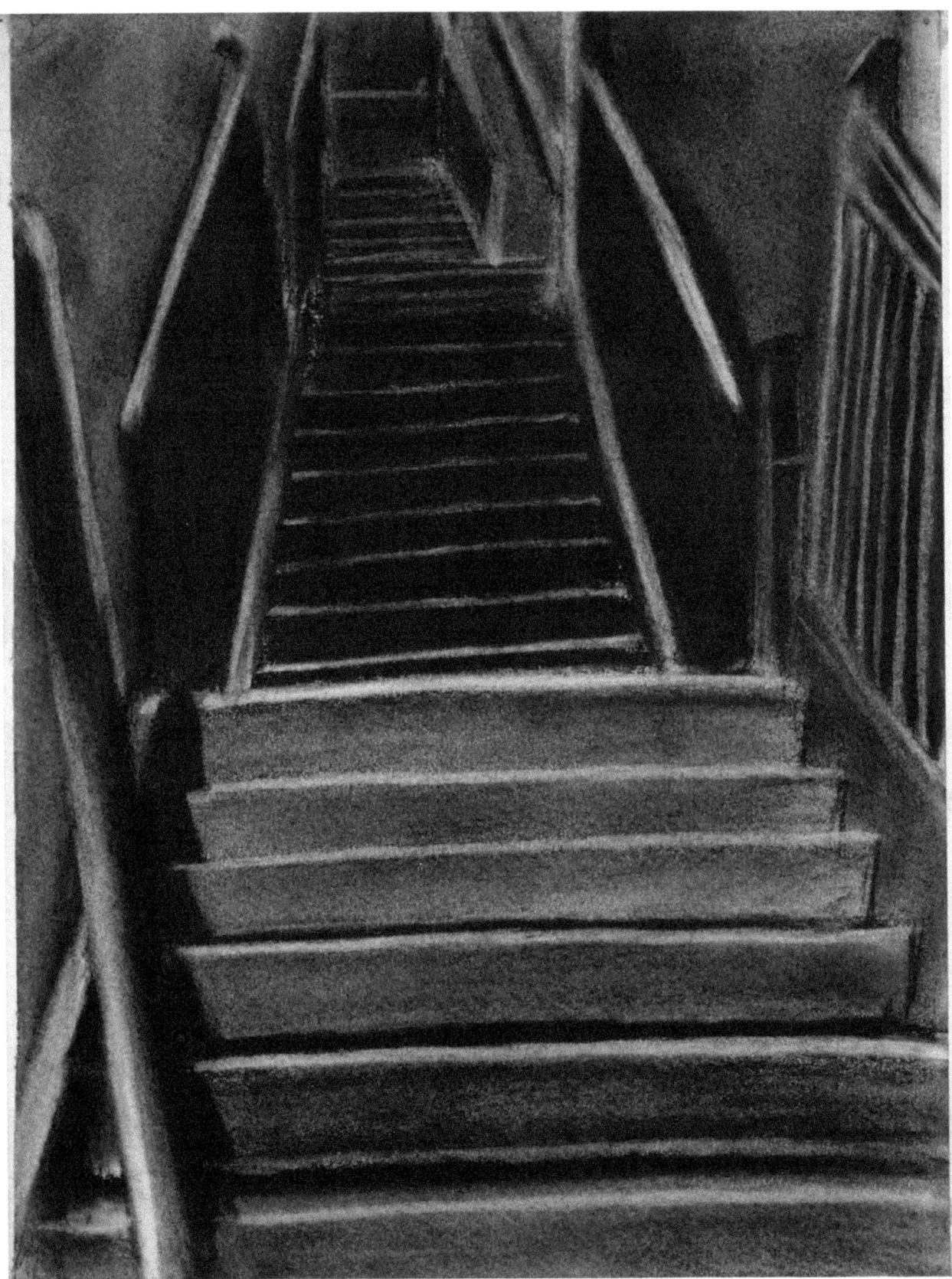

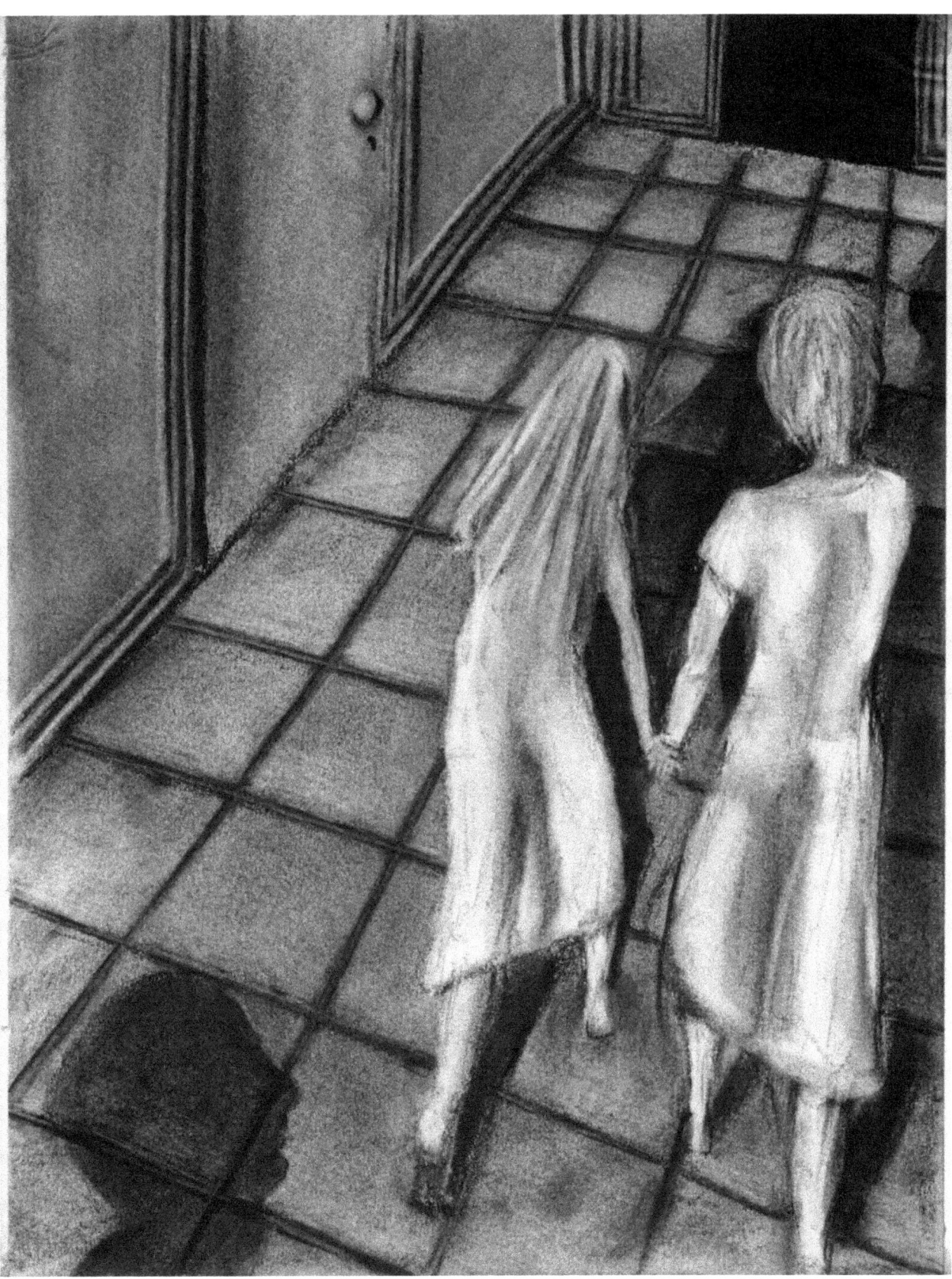

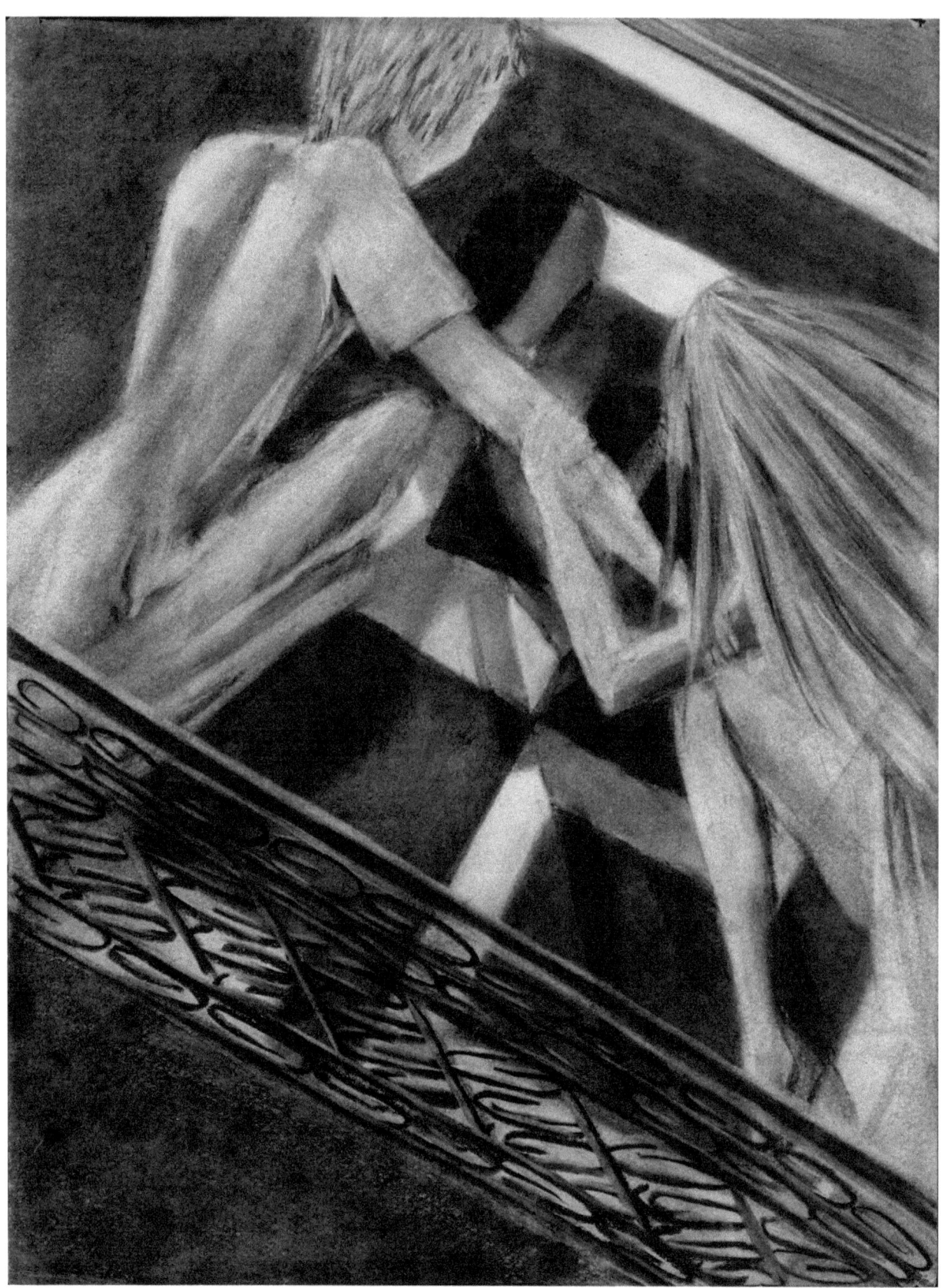

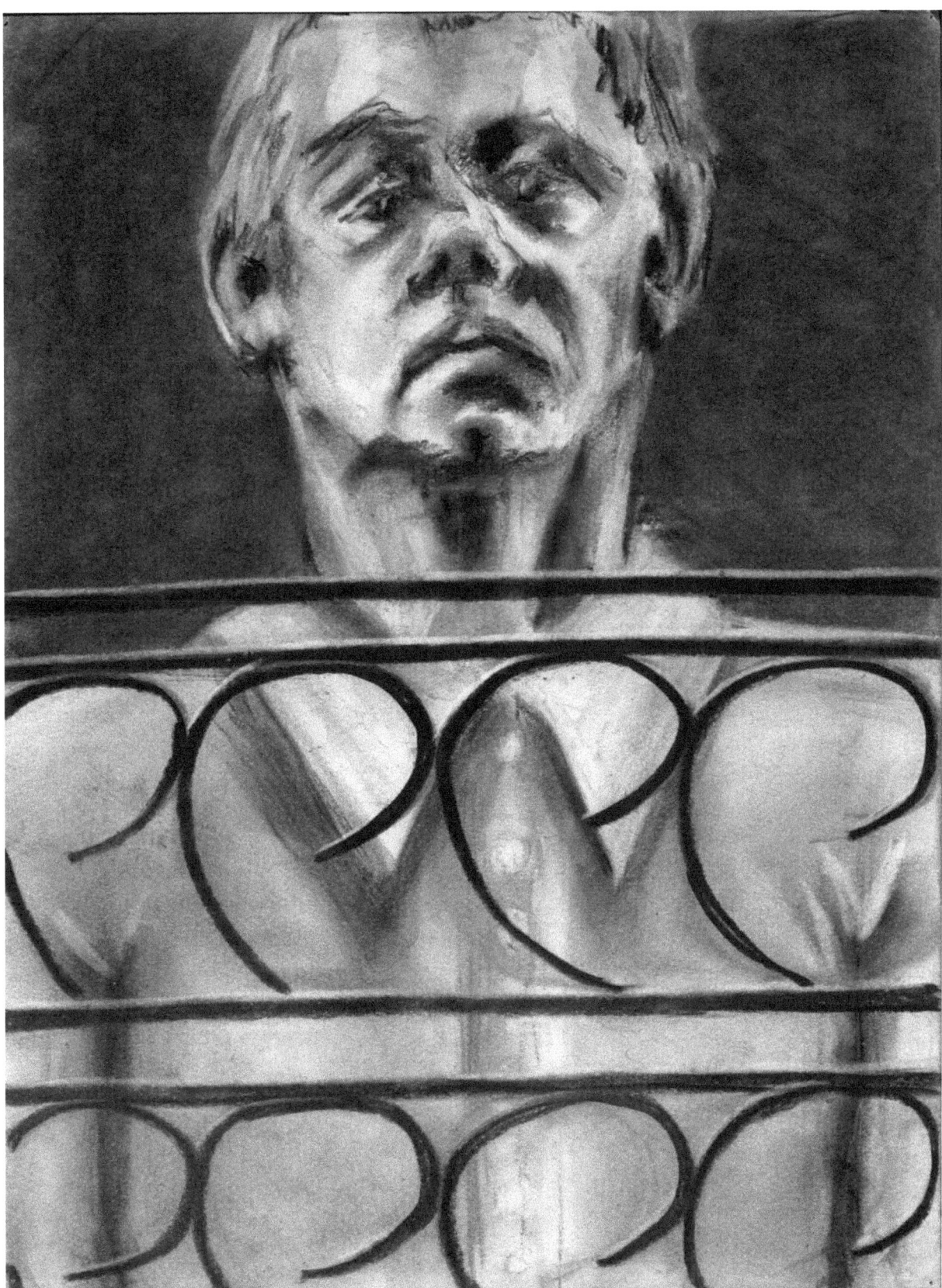

Where are we now, we ask the voices

Who sing their sad song so sweetly.

We reach our arms out,

Only to feel icy water lapping

Against our empty breasts.

Where is the other?

Scan the sky Scan the sky, taunt the voices.

But we were three, we shout.

Dreamers Dreamers Dreamers chant the voices.

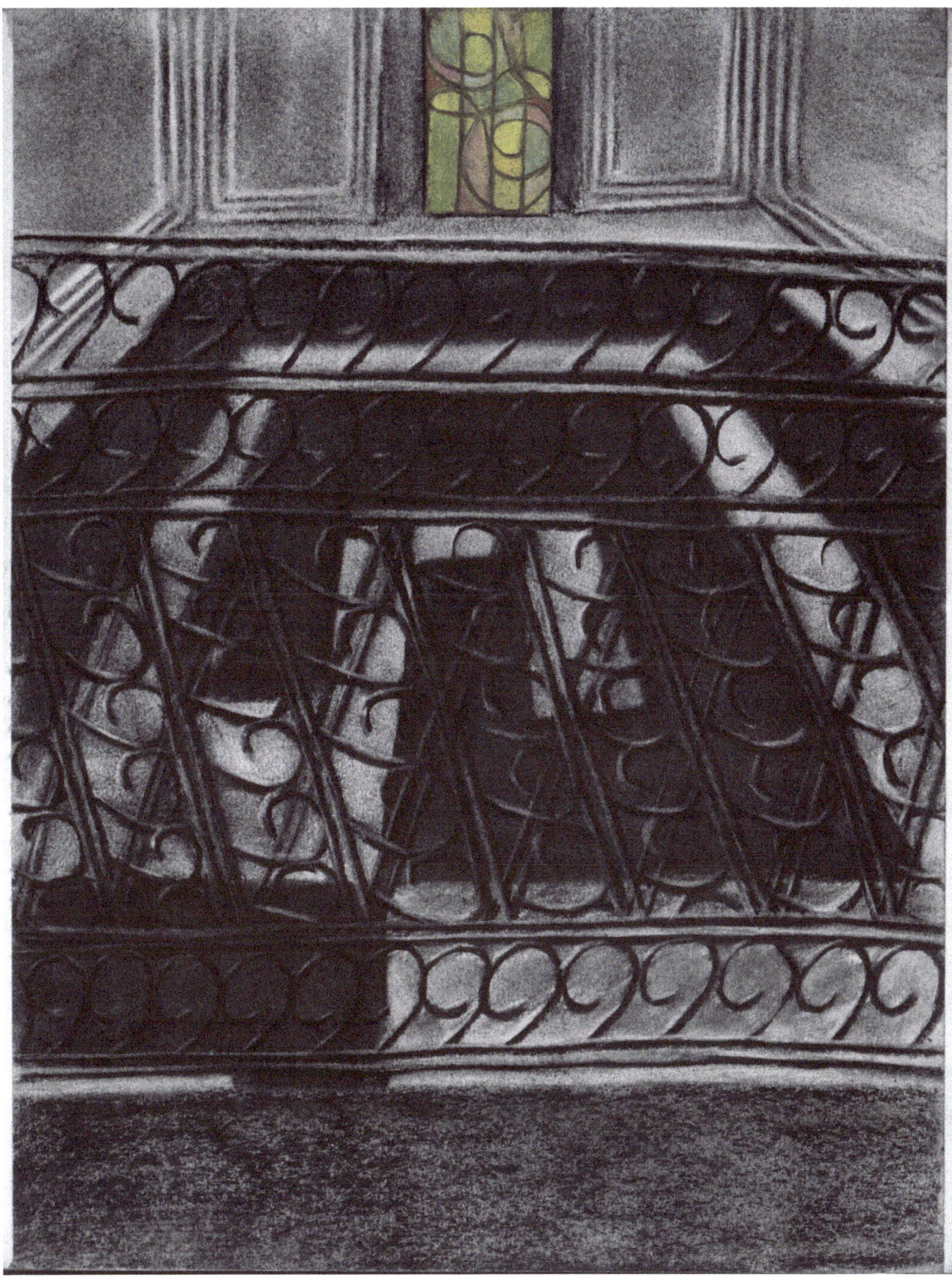

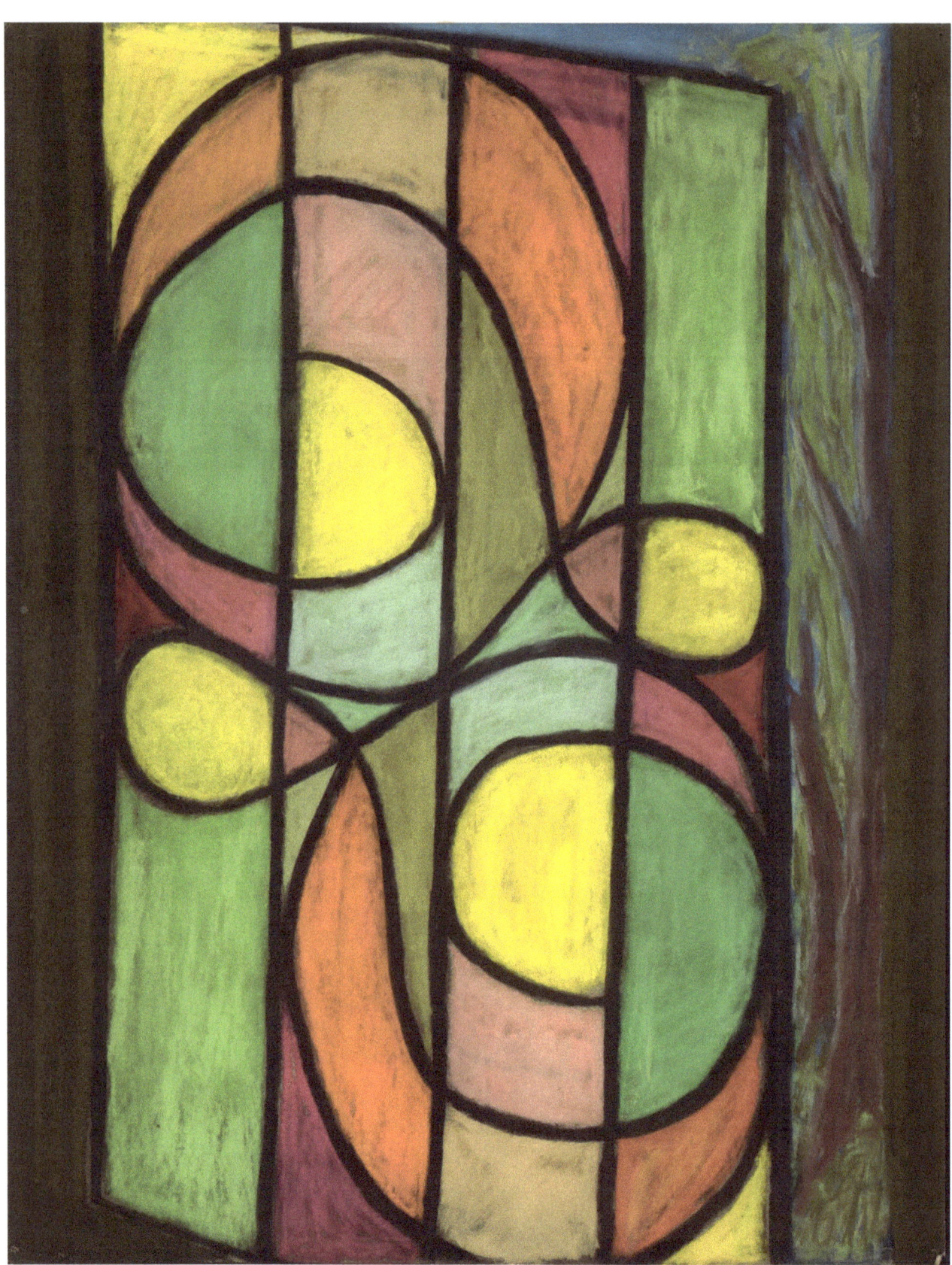

The currents toss us and tease us

As the voices sadly repeat their mournful refrain,

This is all there is This is all there is.

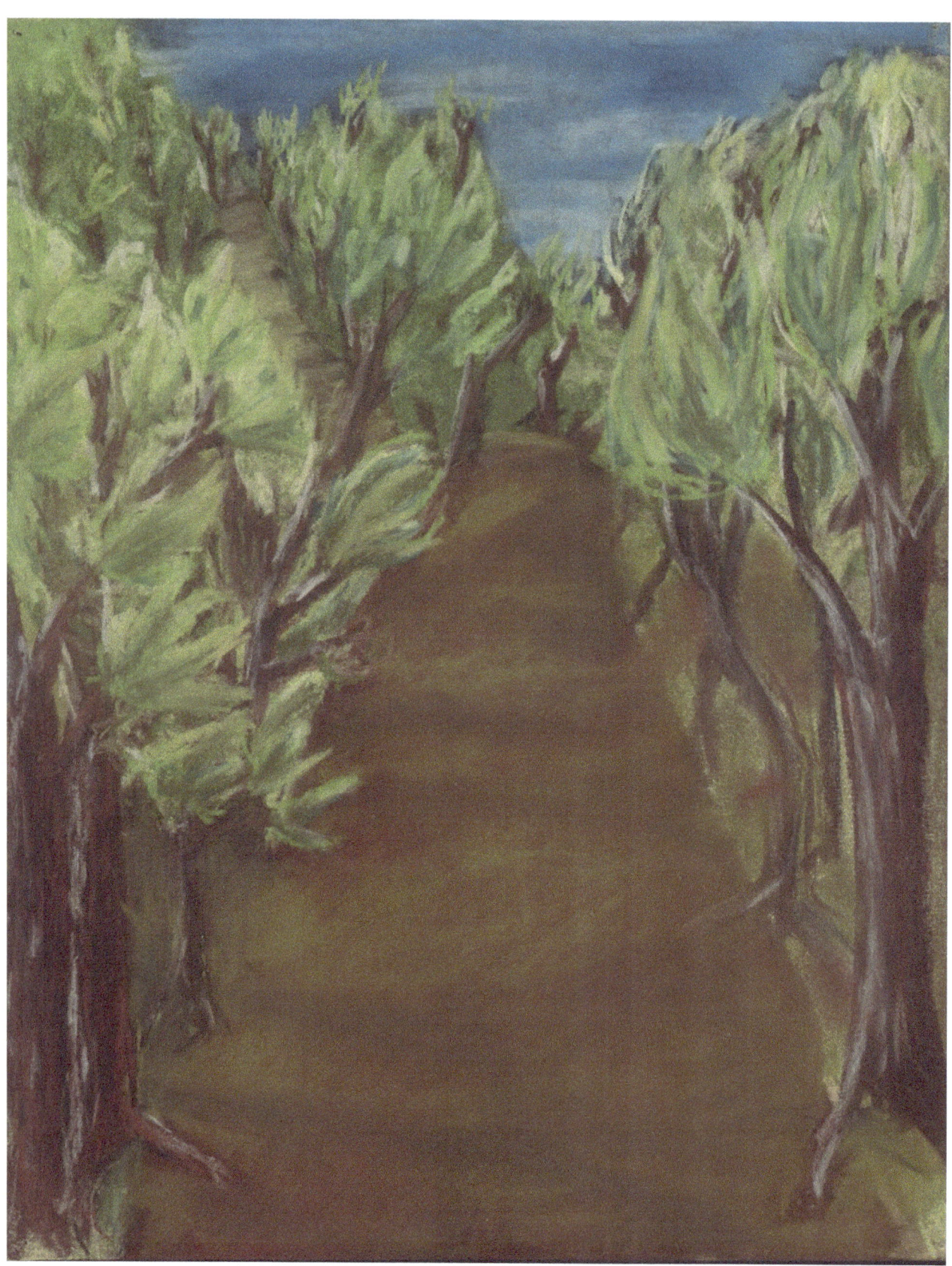

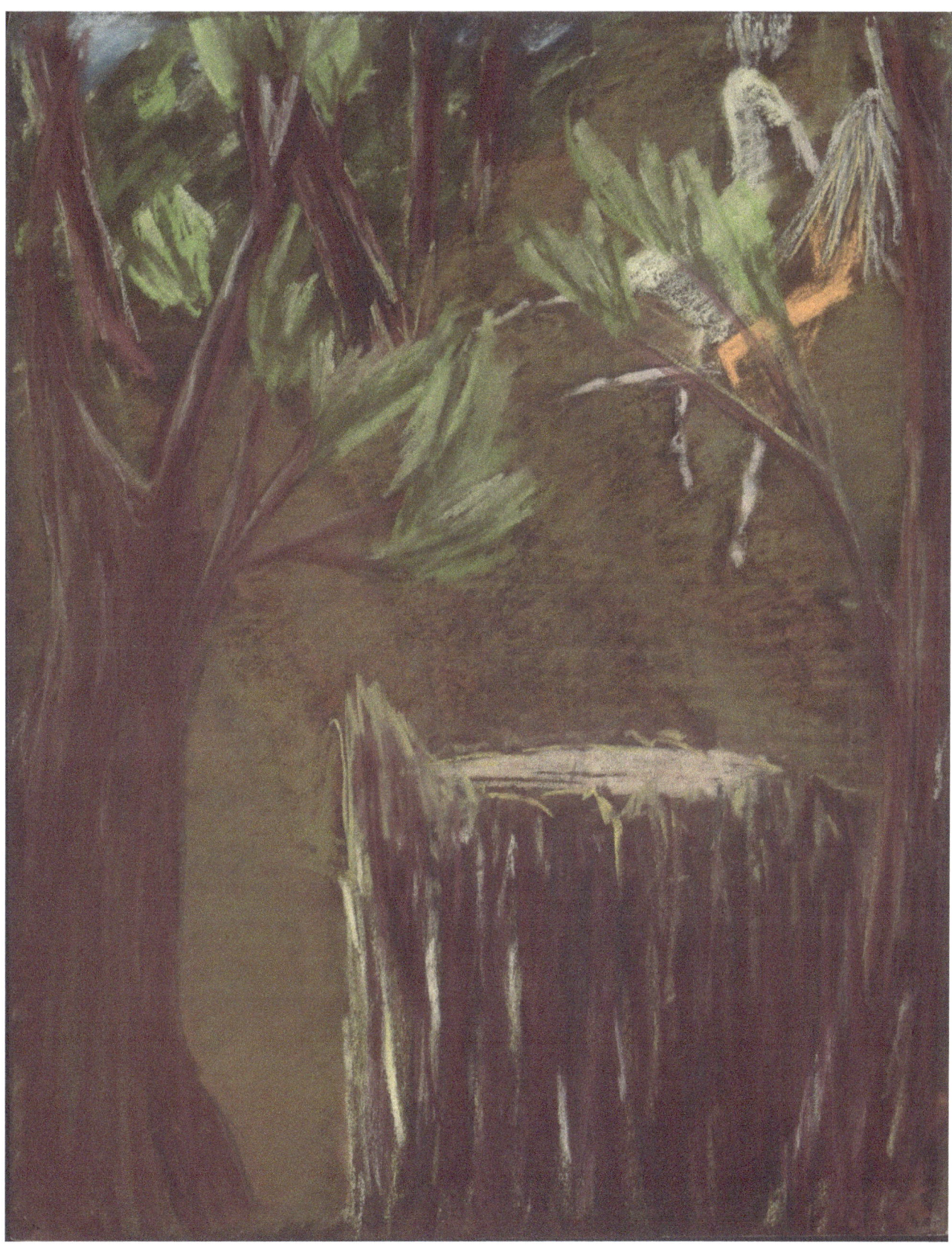

Seek the sky Seek the sky
There is no sky.
The voices wind in and out of each other
With a whisper we strain our ears to hear
And an answering thunder
That fills us.

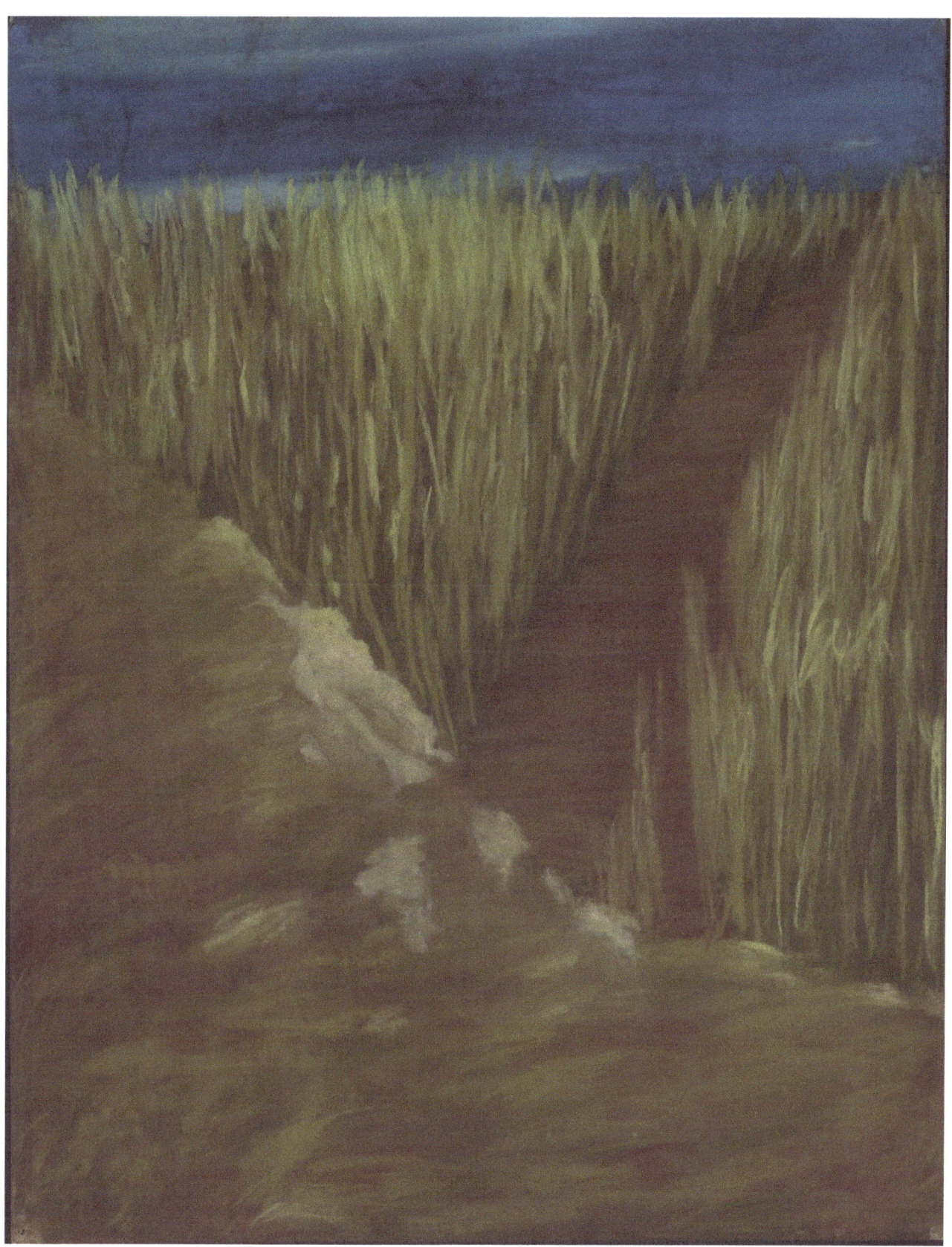

We can just make out the words,

Do not dream again

Do not dream again.

We try to dance to stay awake,

But the music is so slow, so soothing

And we sleep.

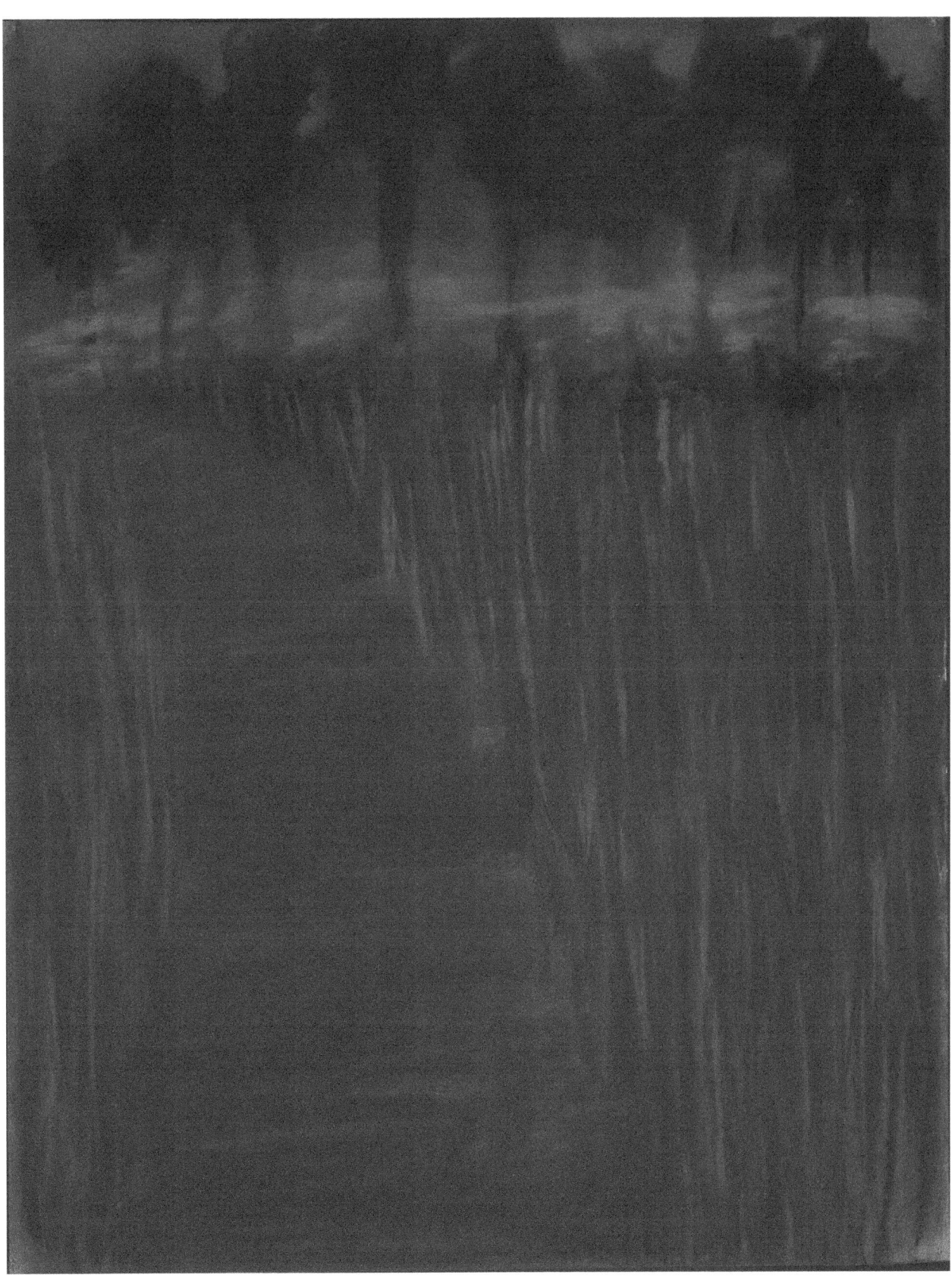

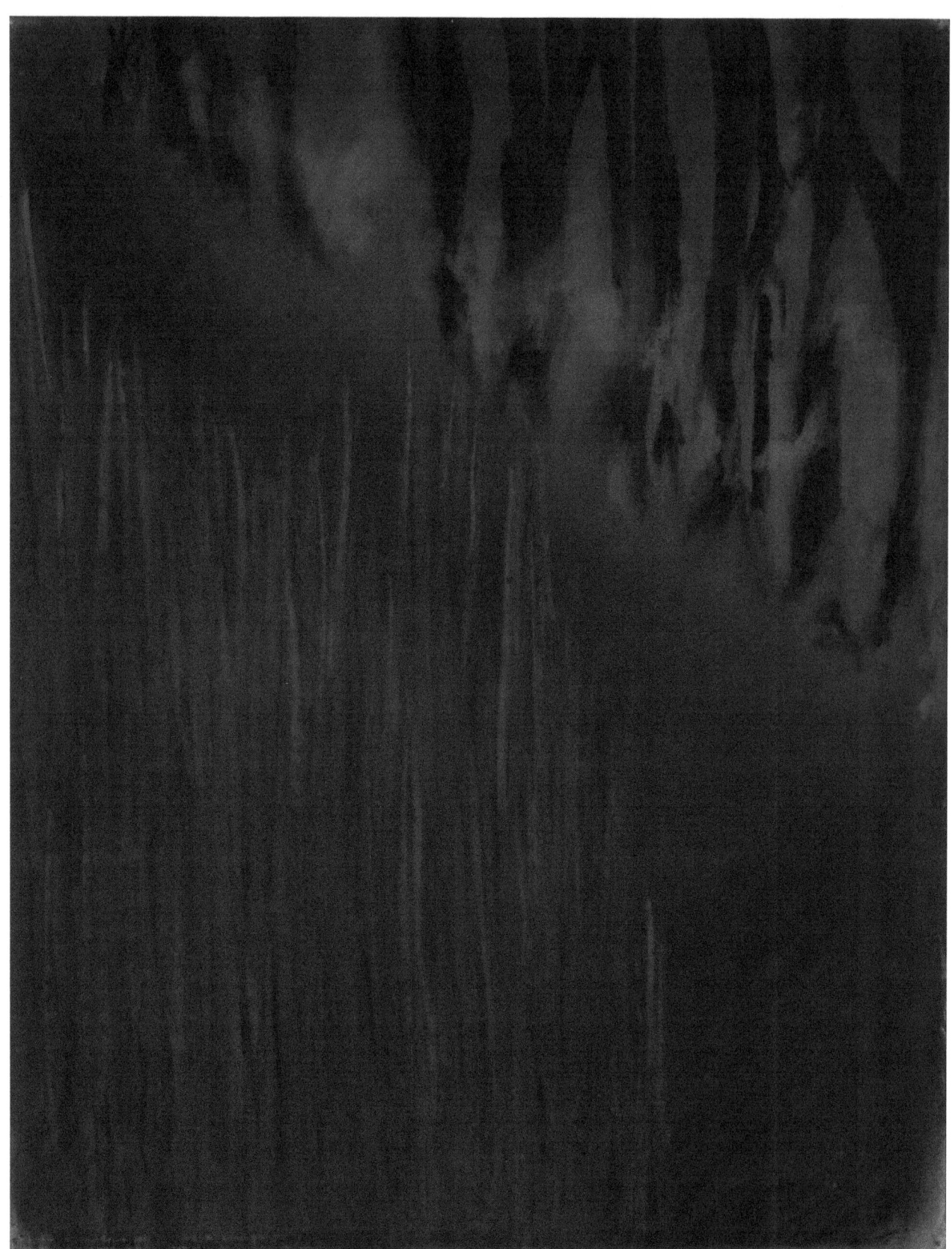

And we dream that we are in

Stagnant waters

Sluggishly we drift through

The thick dank darkness.

We are empty, silent, asleep.

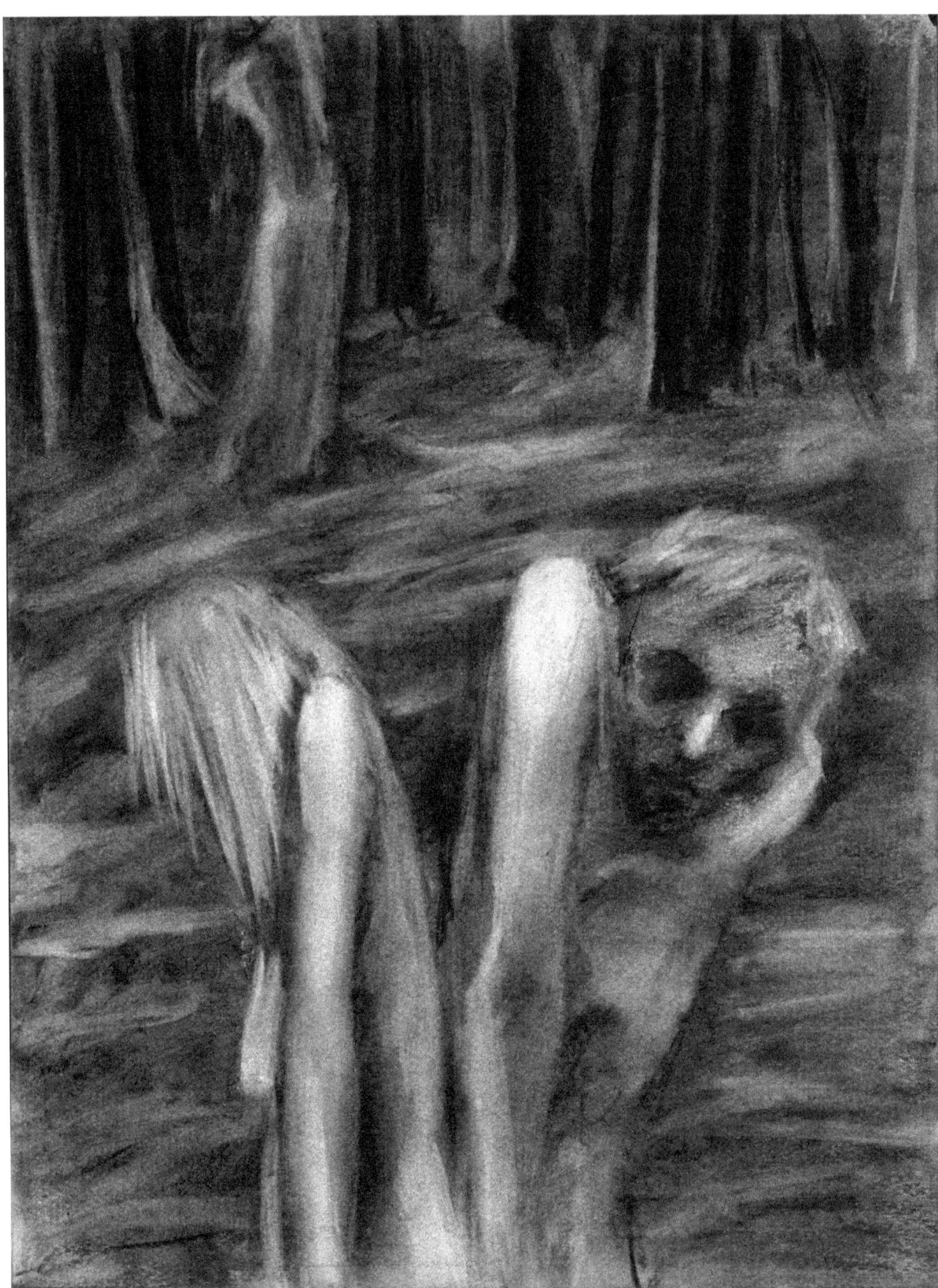

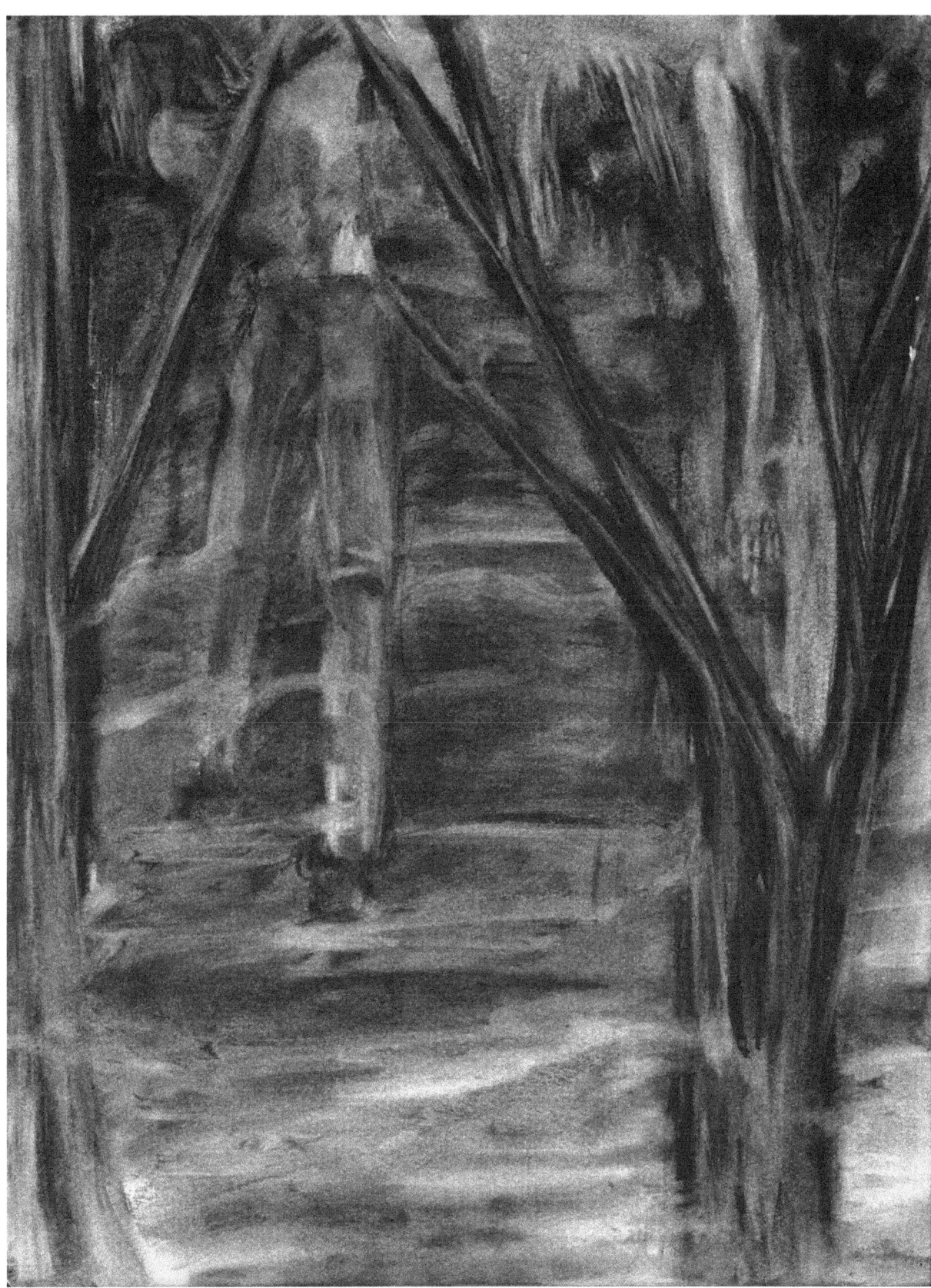

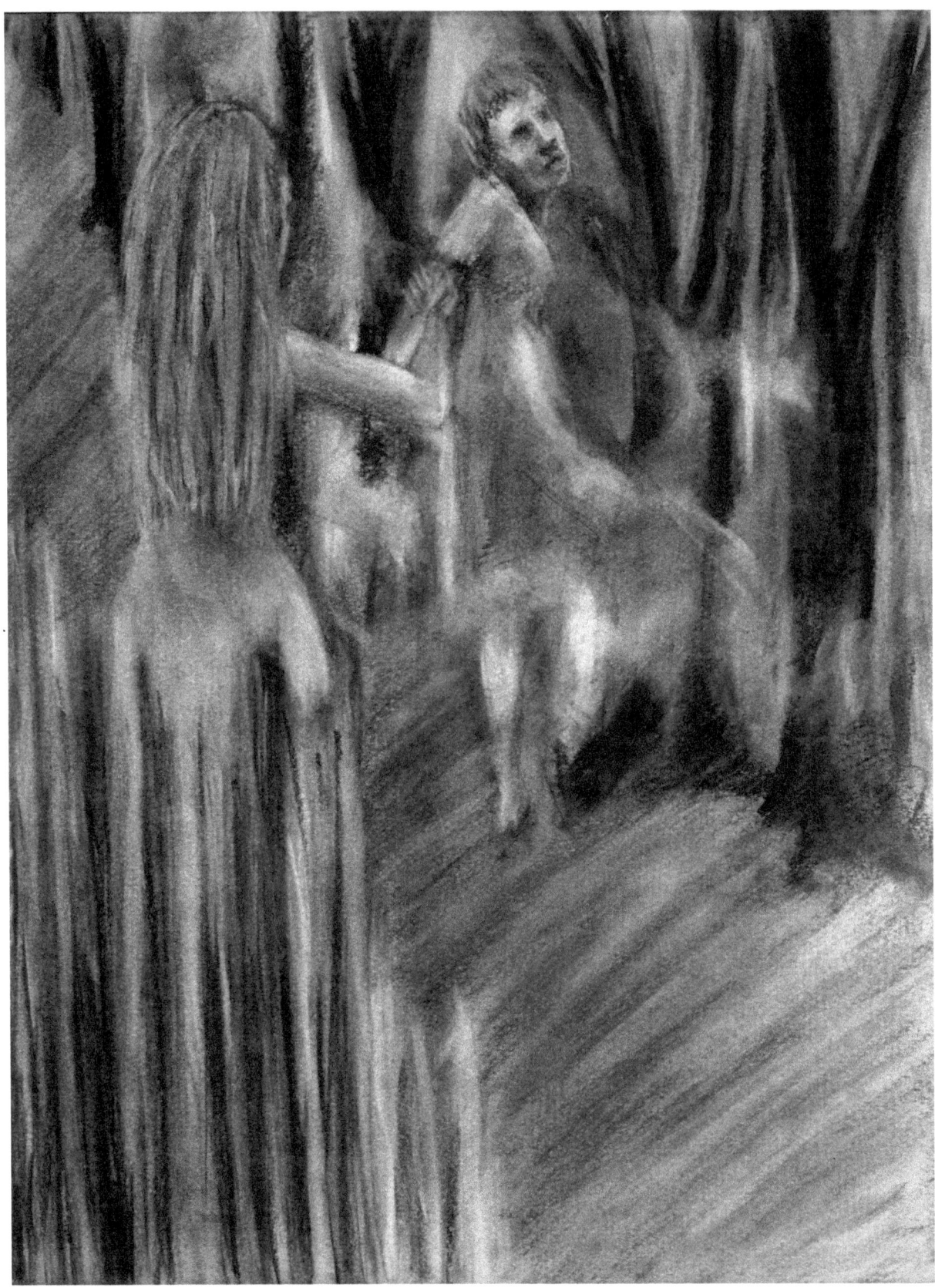

And she begins to drift away,

Dissolving into the murky haze

That surrounds us,

She is water,

She is foam.

She is mist,

I want to seek the sky! I shout,

And we are jarred awake,

As I clasp her shadow to me.

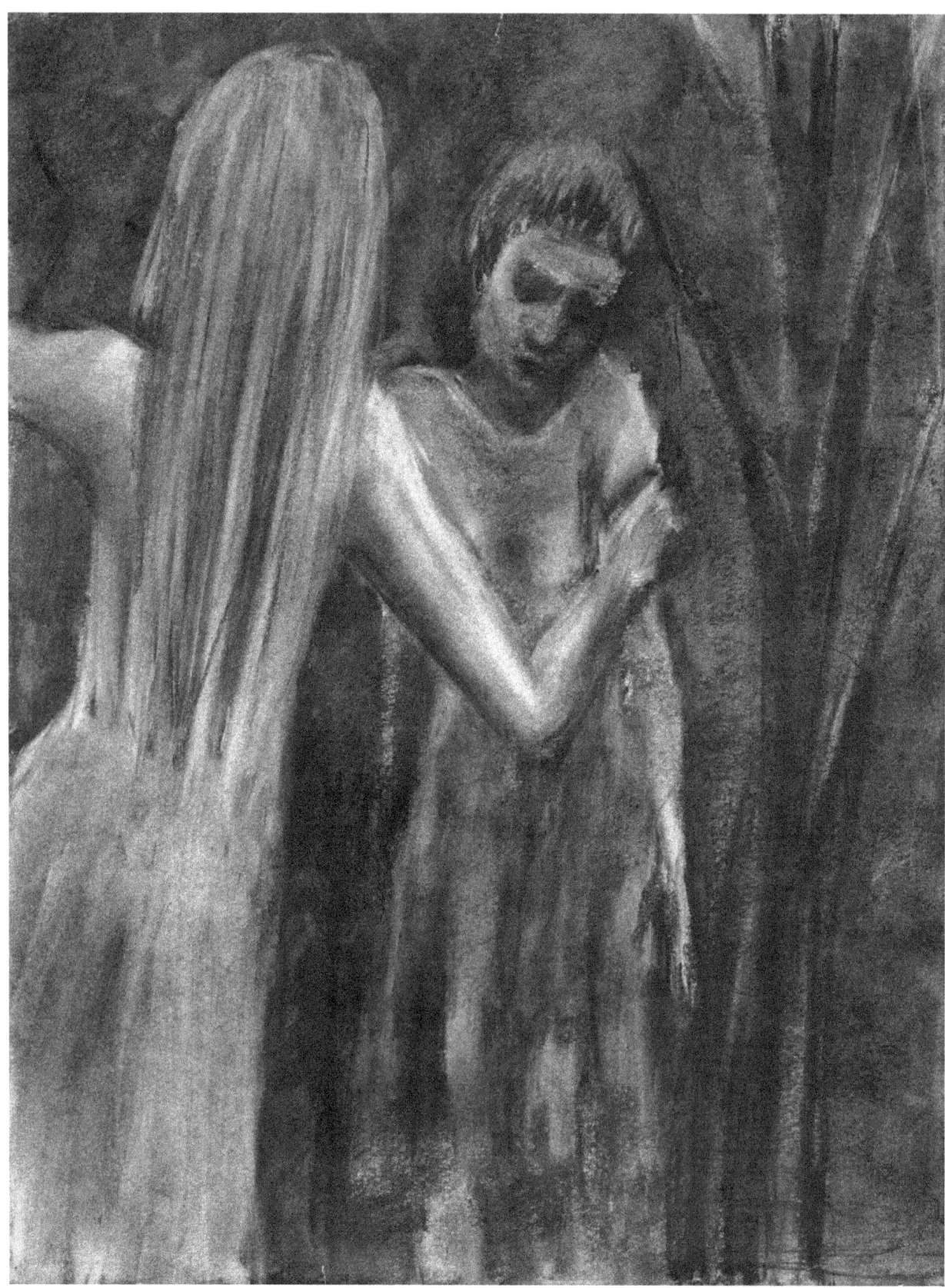

We try to grasp this wave

As the water gently slips through our fingers.

As we listen to the voices sadly say

This is all there is This is all there is.

We swim slowly upward

Toward the sky.